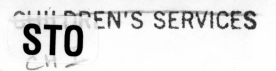

Strange Creatures That Really Lived

Strange Creatures

by **Millicent Selsam**

illustrations by **Jennifer Dewey**

That Really Lived

SCHOLASTIC
HARDCOVER

SCHOLASTIC INC., New York

To Jim
— *M.E.S.*

For E.K.A.
— *J.D.*

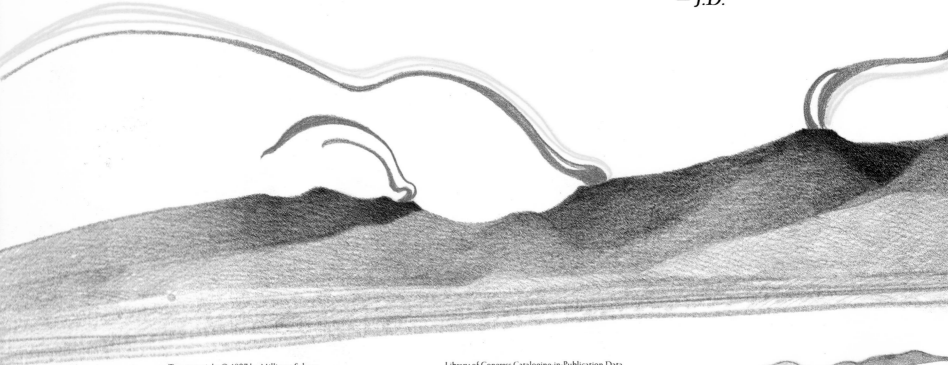

Library of Congress Cataloging-in-Publication Data
Selsam, Millicent Ellis,
Strange creatures that really lived.
Summary: Introduces some animals that lived
long ago, such as the giant sloth, camelus, huge roaches, and uintatherium.
1. Vertebrates, Fossil—Juvenile literature.
[1. Prehistoric animals] I. Dewey, Jennifer, ill.
II. Title.
QE842.S45   1987   560   86-29732
ISBN 0-590-40707-4

12 11 10 9 8 7 6 5 4 3 2 1   7 8 9/8 0 1 2/9
Printed in the U.S.A.   23
First Scholastic printing, October 1987.

Strange animals have always lived on Earth.

Some, like the dinosaurs, lived on land.

6

Other queer animals lived in the sea.
Some looked like fish,
and some looked like lizards.
Others looked like turtles with very long necks.

Strange-looking animals flew through the air, too.

One of the largest of the flying animals was the *pteranodon* (ter-<u>an</u>-o-don).
It looked like a huge bat with leathery wings.
It could glide down from the sky and with its long bill
snatch fish from the sea waves.
It lived seventy million years ago.

Many other strange animals lived long ago.
Archelon (<u>ar</u>-ka-lon) was the largest turtle
that ever lived.
It was twelve feet long — about the size of a car.
It weighed six thousand pounds!
It had a hooked beak and huge flippers.
Its bones were found in South Dakota.
Twenty-five million years ago,
South Dakota was covered by water.
Archelon lived in that inland sea.

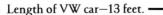
Length of VW car—13 feet.

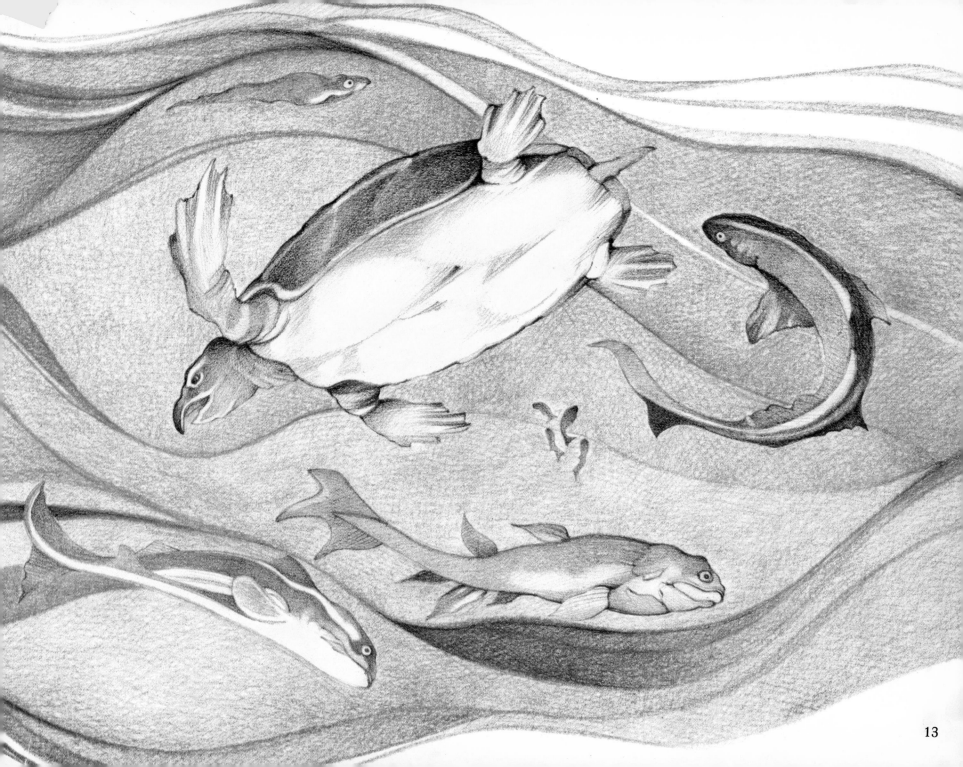

14

Here is another strange animal —
a colossal crocodile (<u>crok</u>-o-dile)
longer than a school bus!
Two hundred million years ago, it roamed
swamps and riverbanks all over the world.
It snapped up any animal that came close to shore.
The largest crocodiles today are dwarfs
compared to the fifty-foot body of this animal.

The *archaeopteryx* (ar-kay-<u>op</u>-ter-icks) looked like
a small dinosaur with feathers.
Scientists think it might have been the first bird
ever to exist. It lived one hundred forty million years ago.
It had a tail and rounded wings.
It also had teeth in its jaws. No bird today has teeth.
Did it fly? Did it glide from tree to tree?
Scientists are not sure.
Archaeopteryx may be the missing link
between scaly reptiles and feathered birds.

Six horns on its head!
Here is an animal as strange as any dinosaur.
Its name was *uintatherium* (yoo-in-ta-<u>ther</u>-ee-um).
It was about the size of an elephant.
Its sharp teeth made it look scary, but scientists
have discovered that it ate only plants.
Sixty million years ago, it thundered over the plains
of the American West.

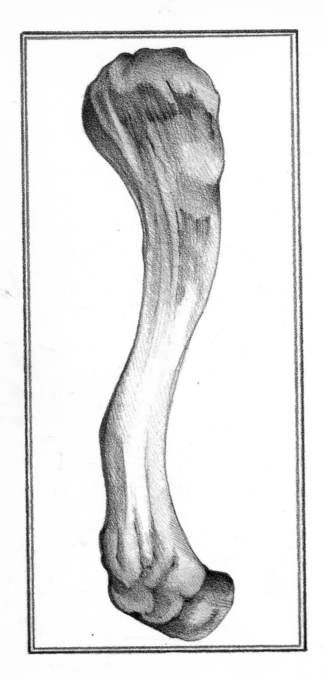

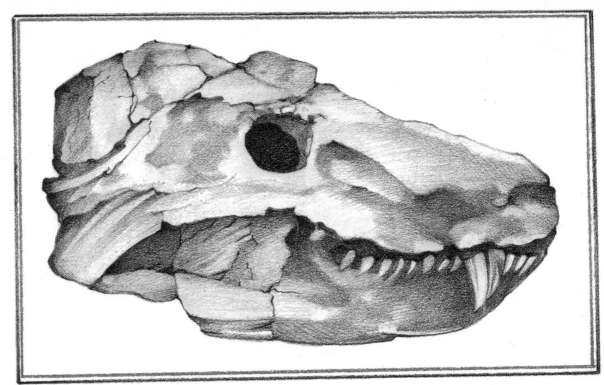

Huge animals once lived in South America.
About one hundred years ago,
a scientist named Charles Darwin found their bones.
Other scientists put the bones together
so they could see what these animals looked like.

One of these animals was a giant land *sloth* (slawth).
It looked like a great hairy bear.
It was as tall as a telephone pole.
From its flat teeth, you can see that it ate plants.
Scientists think it pushed over trees
to get at the leaves in the upper branches.
There are no such sloths alive in the world today.
The last giant sloths died one million years ago.
But we can find their relatives
in Central and South America —
the slow-moving sloths
that hang upside down in the treetops there.

This animal was called the "stabbing cat"
because it had enormous teeth shaped like daggers.
It used its teeth to stab and kill its prey.
Fifty thousand years ago, many cats of this kind
walked into tar pits and were trapped there.
Their flesh decayed, but their bones remained.

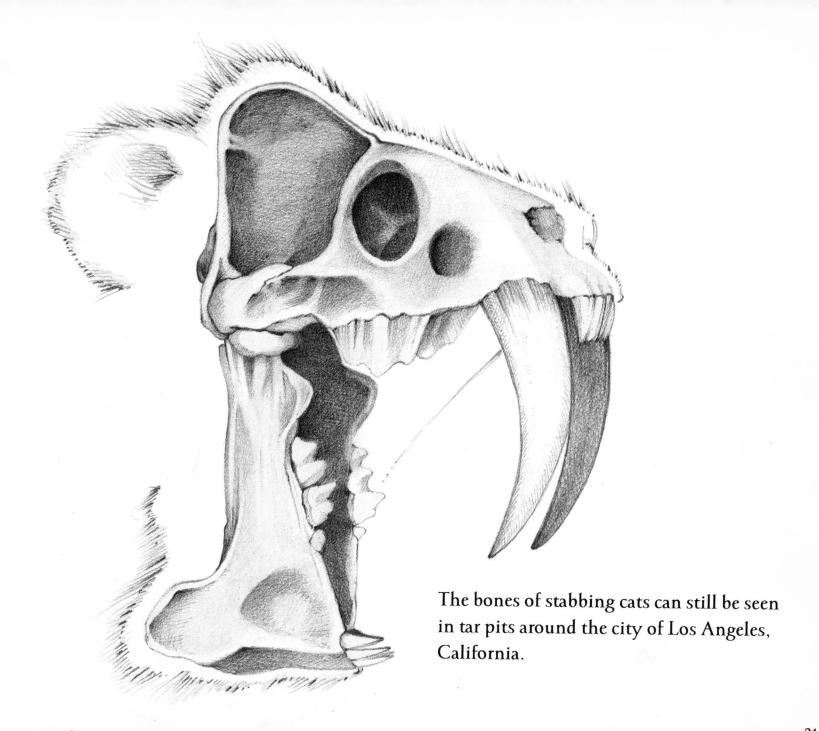

The bones of stabbing cats can still be seen in tar pits around the city of Los Angeles, California.

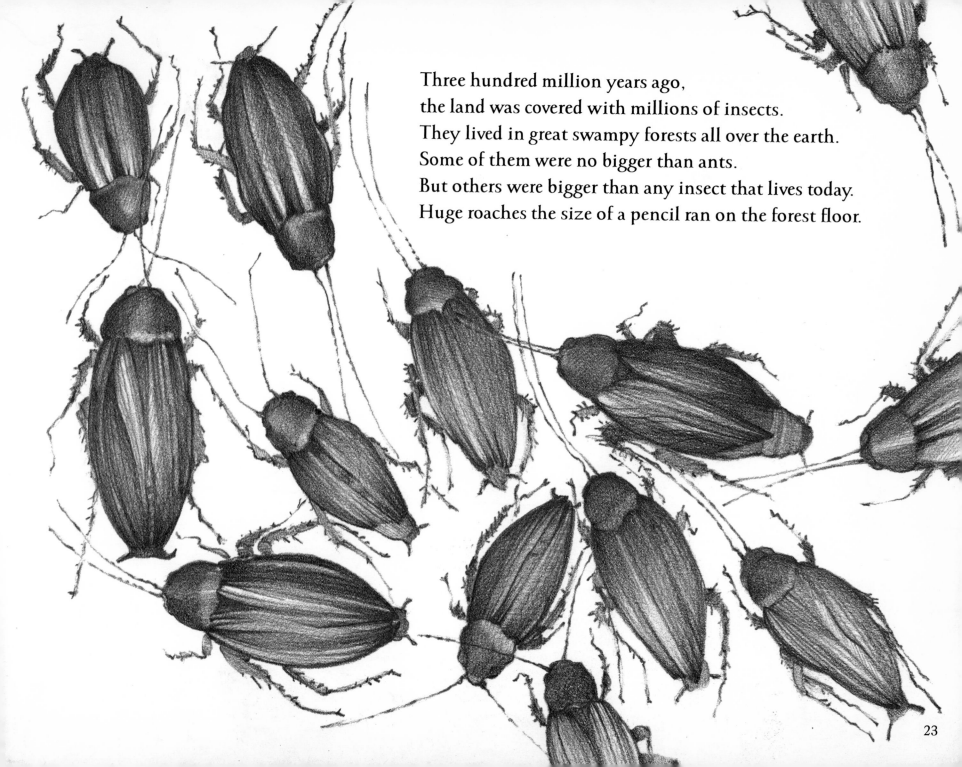

Three hundred million years ago,
the land was covered with millions of insects.
They lived in great swampy forests all over the earth.
Some of them were no bigger than ants.
But others were bigger than any insect that lives today.
Huge roaches the size of a pencil ran on the forest floor.

23

Giant-sized dragonflies flew overhead like kites.

In later times — forty to fifty million years ago —
there were great pine forests.
Sticky resin oozed from the cracks in the trees,
and many small insects got caught in it.
When the resin hardened, it turned into clear amber.
When we look inside that amber today,
the insects seem as though
they might still be alive.
But of course they are not.

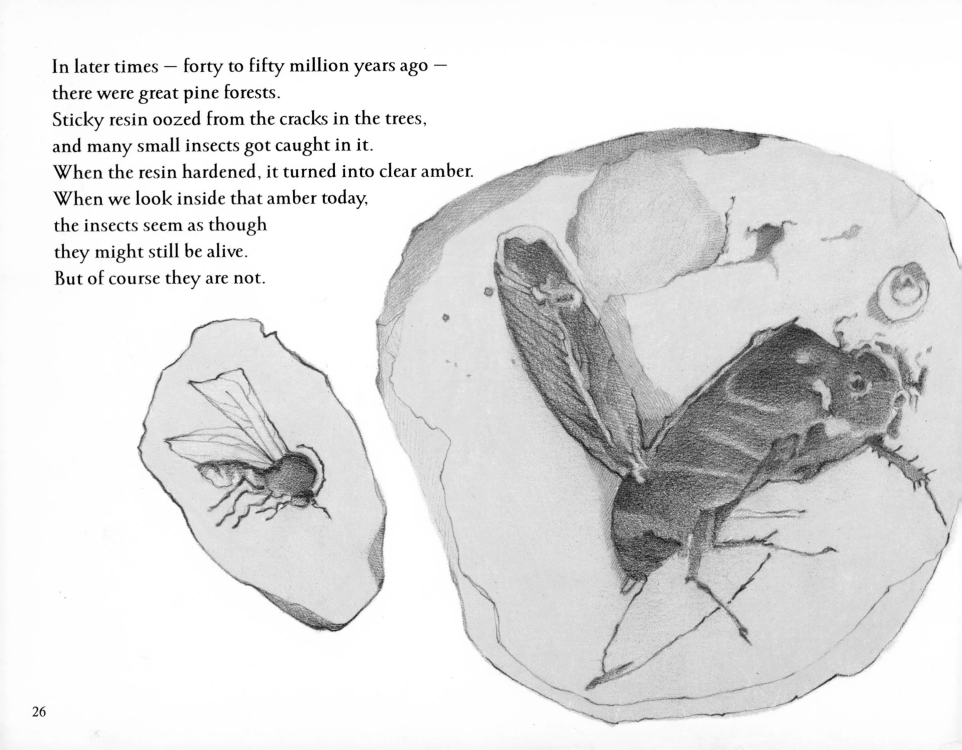